Chinese Pheasants, Oregon Pioneers

VIRGINIA C. HOLMGREN

OREGON HISTORICAL SOCIETY

Oregon State Game Commission photo

Chinese Pheasants, Oregon Pioneers

Virginia C. Holmgren

North, south, east and west across American woodlands the sight of a Chinese ringnecked pheasant may bring a gourmet tingle to the tongue, a gunner's salute to worthy trophy or simply the quickened pulse of pleasure at the beauty of the cock's gold or jewel-toned plumage, the hen's opalescent acorn mottling. But in Oregon anyone with an eye for history frames the pheasant in a special aura, for the birds make a monument in feathers, a living marker on the Oregon pioneer trail. From the Orient to Oregon the pheasants came to make this northwest corner their first sure foothold on American soil.

Few histories, bird guides or reference books show with certain citing of place and date and sponsor that Oregon is the land of the pheasants' American beginnings. The pheasant is South Dakota's official state bird, the reference books may note, or add with bland half-truth that it is a game bird "common in eastern U.S."

The Oregon claim has become so clouded with the passing years that it seems high time the facts were set down and the full tale told of how Chinese ringnecked pheasants first exchanged Oriental haunts for Oregon homestead in the years 1881 to 1884, sponsored by Owen Nickerson Denny and his wife Gertrude Jane. One fact to begin with is this: in the year 1880 Owen Denny of Oregon was consul-general for the United States in the Chinese city of Shanghai. There he and Gertrude made full acquaintance with pheasant beauty in the wild and pheasant flavor on the tongue. They saw, they tasted and they asked themselves with wondering, hopeful breath if these birds of China could breed and thrive in Oregon. Would the ringnecked pheasants make successful Oregon pioneers?

To Owen and Gertrude both, the hardships of pioneering were well known. They had both come west as children—Gertrude as an impressionable ten-year-old; Owen at fourteen. They could judge the pheasants' pioneer trials by their

Owen Denny (OHS Collections)

own, Owen thought. A fourteen-year-old didn't forget how strange a new land could seem.

His birthplace was in Ohio's Morgan County near the town of Beverly; the date, September 4, 1838. Heritage of both New England and South mingled in his veins, for his father, Christian Denny, was a Virginian, and his mother, Eliza Nickerson Denny, could trace her ancestry back to the earliest settlers in Massachusetts. The two had met and married in Ohio—on the last Thursday in September, 1828—and had three sons and three daughters by the year 1852 when they decided to pack up and take the Oregon Trail.

The Dennys had three wagons pulled by twelve yoke of oxen, with about twenty-five head of loose cattle to follow along behind and keep fourteen-year-old Owen and his brothers busy with their care. There were fourteen wagons in the train all told, and Christian Denny had been elected captain. It was an uneventful trip, with no Indian raids or unlooked-for hardships, but it was agonizingly slow. March . . . April . . . May . . . June . . . July . . . August . . . September . . . . They finally got to the Linn County town of Lebanon shortly after Owen's birthday, September, 1852, the land records show.

They looked for trouble to strike on the trail out, and it had spared them, but now here where they thought trouble was done with, it lashed out at them full force. The first thing, Christian was hard-kicked by an Indian pony he tried to tame, and the wound wouldn't heal. Weakened as he was by infection, he fell easy prey to the mountain fever that was going the rounds in Lebanon that fall, and even with Eliza's care he just couldn't shake it. He died about October 20th.

The mimeographed transcript of genealogical data from land claim records gives the year of his death as 1853, but that is an error. Other accounts often mention how heartbreakingly soon after arrival death came—a matter of days, weeks—and the arrival year was 1852. The widowed mother, with six children to provide for, took out her land claim as planned on acreage just west of Lebanon village limits, and it was set down as issued to: "Denny, Eliza, widow of Christian

Denny, deceased, Linn County. Born 1810/11, Massachusetts. Arrived Oregon 25/30 September 1852."

Records say her claim was settled in February of 1854, although there was some confusion about the boundary lines that had to be taken to law later. The difficulty was finally settled 24 October 1864 with a land office document that bore Owen's signature, and his name testified to both a son's and a lawyer's responsibility.

Owen had early chosen the law for his profession. He had helped earn his way through Lebanon Academy and then through Willamette College, and he acquitted himself with a good record in both schools. After graduation he read law under Amory Holbrook in Oregon City and then with the firm of Wilson and Harding in Salem, and passed the state bar examination in 1862. Now, to begin putting his training to the proof, he moved east of the Cascades to that busy town on the Columbia known as The Dalles and joined the staff of C. R. Meigs, prosecuting attorney for the Fifth District. There his work came to the attention of Governor A. C. Gibbs, and when a Wasco County judgeship fell vacant, Owen was appointed to fill the unexpired term. It was wartime, and North-South lines were drawn as sharply in The Dalles as on eastern battlefields. Owen was outspokenly Northern, firmly Republican, a member of the Union League. Some of his letters to the governor written in these days of high feeling have been preserved in the files of the Oregon Historical Society. In one he brands a congressional candidate as "copperhead" and worse: "O shame where is thy blush! Just think of a hog in paradise and then think of this man in Congress. Do, for God's sake, think of our country!"

Now a chance to advance himself with private enterprise took Owen to the Boise mines in Idaho for some six months, but when he returned to The Dalles he again held his former judgeship, this time by election, and he served the full four-year term until 1868 when both business and pleasure urged him to move to Portland.

The pleasure was of the kind that comes accompanied by the sound of wedding bells and toasts and good wishes. He had known Gertrude Jane Hall White for some time and had the good sense not to be intimidated by the fact that she was a divorcee. To him it was much more important that she had a good store of common sense well tempered with twinkling humor and that she seemed miraculously endowed with the ability to stand up to fortune, good or bad.

They were married in Vancouver, Washington Territory, two days before Christmas, 1868. Friends used to recall that Capt. Leonard White, Gertrude's divorced husband and one of the famous Columbia River pilots, asked around to make sure "this Denny fellow" would make the right sort of husband for Jane—as he always called her. Doubtless he was thinking of the sort of stepfather Owen would be for twelve-year-old Nettie, too. Evidently Owen's character stood up to inquiry, for Captain White went back to his river-boating and made no objection.

There had been two children in Gertrude's first marriage. Judd, her firstborn, had drowned at Celilo when he was only nine, in June 1863. He fell off the wharf trying to haul in a big fish and couldn't make out against the Columbia's swift current. The daughter had been named Fonetta by Leonard as a sort of living memorial to his own strong persuasion for "fonetic" spelling, but the oddity had long since been shortened to familiar Nettie when Owen and Gertrude Jane were married. The child was to love both father and stepfather all her life and would pass on tales of both in the years to come when she would marry Bernard Orme Scott and have children of her own.

Meanwhile, Owen was tempted to start his new married life in a new state, and for a year or so he practiced law in San Jose, California. By 1870 he was back in Portland where he was elected police court judge, and forever after bore a judge's title as part of his name. But there were higher rewards for men of Judge Denny's caliber, and in 1874 he received President Grant's appointment as Collector of Internal Revenue for Oregon and Alaska; the next year he was offered the post of consul in Amoy, China. Much as he wanted to try a foreign diplomatic post, Denny refused in order to fulfill his obligations as collector. By 1877, however, he was free to accept the berth of consul in Tientsin, and efficiency soon promoted him to the post of consul-general, with a fine house in Shanghai. There he and Gertrude sat down to that memorable meal of roast pheasant and asked each other the great question: would pheasants breed in Oregon, establish themselves as native wild birds?

Few of their friends in Shanghai seemed to think the venture would succeed. Ringnecks are an independent sort, the oldtimers argued, that can't endure caging, can't stand a sea voyage. A regular chorus of "can't" seemed to meet the Dennys at every turn. Nobody ever wrote it down, but it's not unlikely that Gertrude met the arguments with a forthright, "Don't tell me *can't* till you try!"

Can't was a word for which her practical, common-sense nature had small patience. She had learned about doing the impossible the hard way. Like Owen, she had come to Oregon as pioneer child. Born at Tenmile Run, New Jersey, May 15, 1837, she had been brought West by her parents to the Whitman Mission, where her father, Peter DeSpain Hall, hoped to make a name as architect and builder in the new land. There on November 29, 1847, Gertrude knew the terror of the Whitman massacre, and all her life she was to start at the sound of gunfire or savage yell. She and her mother had been rescued with the other women and children after an eternity that the world outside counted in weeks. But her father, wounded in the first attack, had managed the amazing feat of running to Fort Walla Walla for help. In one of the saddest mistakes of judgment to cloud Northwest history, the fort sentries took him for an Indian rigged in whiteman's disguise and refused to open the gates and let him in or even go out themselves and hear his plea. What did Peter DeSpain Hall think as he staggered back into the forest? Did he die of his wounds or by Indian arrow? The answers will probably never be written, for that was the last anyone ever saw of him, alive or dead. But Gertrude was not forever to be denied a father's care, for her mother later married a man named Robert Beers and there were eventually five little half-sisters to share all of the frontier work and play. The good came with the bad. Gertrude had learned very early

that life held both and that you didn't get far with the word
can't.

Would pheasants make good Oregon pioneers?

"Let's try," said Gertrude Denny.

Owen's enthusiasm leaped higher at her accord. It was like
him to want to learn all there was to know about the birds.
He may have learned that a Portuguese sailor named Fernando Lopez, jumping ship on St. Helena Island in 1573, took
some stolen ringnecks with him and established the breed
there. Perhaps Denny also learned that there had been several unsuccessful attempts to establish pheasants in America.
The first of these trials had been made by Richard Bache,
English-born son-in-law of Benjamin Franklin, who had liberated English blackneck pheasants on his New Jersey estate
along the Delaware River. The birds had ample food and
shelter, but they did not survive. Neither did a later batch
released near Belleville on the Passaic River. Meanwhile,
Governor Wentworth of New Hampshire had introduced
English pheasants on his estate in 1790, but these also failed
to produce a surviving second generation. The Robert Oliver
family of Harewood, near Baltimore, also tried pheasant introduction several times around 1800, but although a few
birds bred in their first season, the flocks did not survive the
winter. Whether the cold, prowling beasts or hungry hunters
had brought disaster, none could say.

All of these unsuccessful transplants were English pheasants, usually called "blacknecks," and it was strange they did
not adapt to the new land, for they themselves were a pioneer
strain brought to England in such remote times that only the
Romans could have been responsible. From the Romans, factual pheasant history can be traced back to the ancient
Greeks, but at some point in the maze of Grecian fact and
fable, provable pheasant history was lost in legend.

According to legend, then, those intrepid voyagers the Argonauts had sailed to the far-east Land of the Golden Fleece
and brought back many a treasure, and among these wonders
was a long-tailed bird of radiant plumage found beside the
river Phasis in the province of Colchis. Wherever the river
Phasis wandered, there were these jewel-toned birds, so the

Argonauts related to their spellbound listeners, and thereafter *phasianos ornis*—the Phasian bird—was the name that went from legend into history as the Greeks carried their long-tailed beauties from Colchis back to Greece. In time, when Roman conquerors took the bird for their own trophy, they kept the Phasian name and carried both bird and word with them as they swept across the conquered lands of Gaul and Goth and Saxon.

The foreign tongues twisted the name somewhat and foreign pens spelled it faisan, faisant, fesaunt and half-a-dozen other ways, but the echo of the mother river Phasis clung to every twisting. In England the spelling became *pheasant*, and when further invasion of Oriental wilds revealed other birds of long tails and jewel-like feathering in different hues—gold, scarlet, silver, jet and green—they, too, were recognized as pheasant kin and given the pheasant name.

In the years after 1735 when the famous Swedish scientist Carl Linnaeus set the whole scientific world to more accurate classifying of all birds, beasts, plants and minerals according to his dictatorial *Systema Naturae*—the system of nature—the Phasian birds came in for systematizing, too. Now the name *pheasant* was no longer sufficient, and they were catalogued by order, family, genus and species like everything else that came under the systematists' scrutiny. "*Pheasant*" might do for a common folk name, but for science there had to be a Latin binomial for each species—the genus title plus the species name—so that no mistake in identity could ever occur.

The order was easy enough to decide—order *Galliformes*, the chicken-like birds. The family would bear their own historic label—family *Phasianidae*—and all pheasant-like birds would be assigned to it, keeping alive the Argonauts' ancient journey to the Golden Land in scientific annals as well as in myth and legend. When these Oriental wonder-birds were further set apart into a sub-family, the name still carried the far-reaching ripples of the river Phasis, for the coinage was *Phasianinae*.

Genus by genus, species by species, the jewel-toned birds have been classified to make sixteen generic divisions. Each has its scientific Latin label, but the English names read: blood pheasants, tragopans, koklas, monals, jungle fowl, gallopheasants, eared pheasants, cheer pheasants, and long-tailed, true, ruffed and peacock pheasants, the crested argus, great argus, peafowls and Congo peacocks.

It is a royal family to belong to, and if the peacock stands first among them in the world's wonder by reason of its great tail plumes and blue-green-gold brilliance, then surely the true pheasants are close in line. And it is to the genus of true pheasants, the genus *Phasianus*, that the Chinese ringneck is assigned by scientific analysis. With it in this classification are four other strains to make five sub-genus divisions: black-necked, white-winged, Kirghiz or Mongolian, Chinese or gray-rumped, and green.

These five races of the same genus all interbreed with fertile offspring when they meet, and they have been able to keep to themselves as separate strains in the Asian wilds only because geographical barriers and lack of manmade roads make meeting infrequent. Each of the five, as it was discovered and classified, was assigned a Latin name by the Linnean systematists. At first a two-part name—to indicate genus and species—was considered sufficient, but as sub-genus distinctions were made, a third part became inevitable. The blacknecked, first-named, was originally *Phasianus colchicus*. Now in trinomial category it became *Phasianus colchicus colchicus*, with repetition showing that it was the prototype for the entire group. The ringneck became *Phasianus colchicus torquatus*, to mark the white torque or neck chain that is one of the bird's outstanding features.

Apparently the original blacknecked pheasants did not have the white torque, but most of the other races in this five-fold genus wear a collar almost as wide and white as that of the ringneck itself. Since these other white-collared birds also come from China, neither "Chinese ringnecked pheasant" nor *Phasianus colchicus torquatus* serves as a name to set this one species apart from all its look-alike cousins. "Gray-rumped pheasant" has been suggested as a more accurate label, for the birds do have a gray-green-blue rump patch which the others lack. But changing the pattern of folk speech has never been easy, and revising Linnean Latin would be a matter for pondering by ornithologists of every country where the ringneck roams. The *torquatus* tag was entered by Gmelin in the 1789 edition of *Systema Naturae* (Volume I, part II, page 742), and is too well established for easy revision now.

Other revisions and additions have been made in pheasant listing whenever new species were discovered. Linnaeus tallied only three pheasant genera and seven species in his revision of 1758. In 1951 Jean Delacour, author of *Pheasants of the World*, accounted for the sixteen pheasant genera now recognized, with forty-nine species, 122 subspecies.

Scientists who like to split hairs have even divided the ringneck strain into seventeen subspecies, each with some small difference in coloring to warrant the distinction. In the scientific passion for clarity—or for getting one's name on record as a discoverer—probably more attention has been paid to such minute differences than is necessary. Furthermore, geographic isolation so that in-breeding can repeat the small differences from generation to generation is now less and less likely, even in the Old World where pheasant divisions began. The sub-family *Phasianinae* spread out from the foothills of the Caucasus on the Black Sea—and perhaps beyond from into Thrace and Bulgaria—roving all across Asia east to Korea and Japan, north to Manchuria. The race we call the ringneck seems to have arisen near the coast and is known from Shantung Province and the Hwang-Ho Valley south to the Tonkinese border, the most abundant of all the true pheasant genus.

Gertrude and Owen Denny may not have known the entire ringneck history, but they knew they had beautiful birds waiting in their Shanghai courtyard for Oregon pioneer journey. With these long-tailed beauties were a few Chefoo partridges and Mongolian sand grouse that had also caught Owen's speculative eye.

The assembling had been hasty, for only in winter when the birds' sex organs are shriveled and functionless would the lusty cocks tolerate a rival in the same cage. So Denny worked quickly, knowing that even if he got the birds aboard by January it would be March before they would arrive in Oregon, and sexual resurgence might begin as early as February. Owen wrote his friend A. H. Morgan, who was to handle pheasant release on Oregon terrain, on January 29, 1881, about final arrangements:

I mentioned in my last that it was my intention to try and stock our State with some of the finest varieties of game pheasants found in China, and to this end I have been collecting them for some months past.

I am sending by the ship *Otago* out of Port Townsend, Captain Royal commanding, about 60 Mongolian pheasants to be turned loose in various sections of the state. . . .

These birds are delicious eating and very game and will furnish fine sport. I also send 11 Mongolian sand grouse. These birds have very peculiarly shaped feet—resembling somewhat those of a mole. Next I send 7—all I could possibly obtain before the ship sailed—Chefoo partridges. I am collecting other varieties which I shall send in due time—some of them beautiful birds.

Will you please cooperate with the sportsmen's clubs and see that due notice is given so that the "shootists" will not kill them?

Please lose no time in setting these birds at liberty as soon as they arrive. . . .

Next I am sending 16 trees of the Pang Tao or flat peach. These trees bear very delicious fruit and will do well in Eastern Oregon. The fruit resembles a tomato. I also send a lot of bamboos. They will need to be planted in a rich, moist, sandy soil where they will get plenty of sun. I do not see why the bamboo should not do well in Oregon.

The bamboo seedlings did do well—quite a few present stands in Oregon and southern Washington can trace their rootage back to the wicker tubs that were stored aboard the *Otago* that January day—but that was not the part of the letter that mattered most for pheasant record. Nor was the actual number of birds sent of lasting significance, although it would later be variously tallied as twenty pairs, eighty birds, thirty-six, fifty-seven. The important factor is that Denny— by a slip of the pen, perhaps—wrote *Mongolian* pheasants, not Chinese ringnecks. *Phasianus colchicus mongolicus,* the so-called Mongolian pheasant, looks much like the ringneck, although its torque is not so wide and white. It has darker body plumage, darker rump patch, but it can be most quickly distinguished from the ringnecks by its white epaulets. The tell-tale shoulder patch on a full-grown ringneck cock is Ming blue.

Denny had probably never seen a *Mongolicus*, for this sub-genus ranges far to the west on Kirghiz steppes. Perhaps the misnomer had somehow been transferred to Shanghai, but it seems much more likely that in the haste to make the mail boat Denny wrote "Mongolian sand grouse" and then inadvertently repeated "Mongolian pheasants." However it happened, the tag was a mistake that the birds themselves could prove to anyone who knew the difference. But no one apparently did know, then. Mongolian was the word first heard and it stuck fast, for the Portland *Oregonian* published Denny's letter to Morgan when the birds finally arrived. There it was for all to read on page 3, column 3 of the March 12, 1881 *Oregonian* . . . "Mongolian pheasants."

Copied by other papers and magazines, quoted as the basic source, the misnomer slipped into common speech in spite of all later attempts at correction. Dictionaries and reference books still list it, apparently with no idea as to how the mistake became so thoroughly fixed. The *Oregonian* repeated it in an article on March 22 (p. 3, col. 1):

Mr. A. H. Morgan received a few days ago from Port Townsend per ship Otago from Shanghai a number of game birds, bamboo roots, etc. sent to his care by Hon. O. N. Denny. The birds were kept in the hold and withstood the trip well. Only a few died; however, in bringing them from Port Townsend to Portland they fared badly. While in the dark vessel they were quiet and unfrightened, but when in train and boats, rattling and splashing scared the birds, which beat and bruised themselves on the bars. Cloth was then placed inside but had to be removed to prevent birds from smothering.

Only 17 of about 50 Mongolian pheasants survived, and 5 out of 7 Chefoo pheasants [*sic*]. The surviving Mongolians were sent to George Green's farm on the Lower Columbia to be turned loose. The Chefoo will also be sent to the country. Also eleven sand grouse reached here in splendid condition and will be sent to Astoria to be turned loose on Clatsop Plains.

Mr. Denny also sent his brother in Linn County 9 Langshan chickens (3 cocks, 6 hens) which were forwarded by express yesterday. This is the first shipment of this breed to Oregon. Roots of bamboo and other plants arrived in splendid condition and will be sent to The Dalles, White Salmon, etc. and planted.

So, there were seventeen Chinese ringneck pheasants—battered and weary from that wild fight for freedom when they caught their first smell of land, their first glimpse of sunlight and fresh air after the tainted pall of the dank hold—battered and weary, but alive. There on Sauvie Island the three hens and fourteen cocks took cautious survey tour of the Green farm, getting their land legs under them again in this strange domain filled with unknown dangers. Later accounts would give varying tally of their total, but most reports agreed that there were just three hens, a ratio completely out of kilter with pheasant custom.

Any pheasant rooster worthy of his harem rights expects to have at least two or three wives in his seraglio, and if there be more, that is so much more to his liking. Apparently with no wife at all, or even only one, the regal rooster loses all of his usual instincts to hold and defend home territory, and roams so far in search of proper mates that his chances of survival practically vanish. Consequently, in order to maintain pheasant survival pattern of large broods watched over by devoted mothers in an established area guarded by zealous cock, the normal cock-to-hen ratio must be kept. And how could that be done in that mismatched pioneer band of fourteen handsome husbands for only three mates?

Perhaps one lusty lover took all three brides, or the division may have been two and one, even one and one. At any rate, a report was later made that two of the hens were seen with broods during the summer. It was only hearsay, recalled some years later when the United States Department of Agriculture would send a representative out to Oregon to investigate pheasant status, but it seems likely enough. The report that some of the foreign birds were also seen at several points on the mainland that winter seems equally reasonable, for the unmated cocks would not have been inhibited by the small water barrier between them and the missing mates that instinct bade them seek. Young cockerels from the summer broods would also have begun fanning out to search for harems of their own by February or March. But rumor and tradition say that none of this first pioneer band survived long enough to be concerned with new springtime matings. The Chefoo partridges and sand grouse had definitely vanished. Word must have gone back to Shanghai that once again pheasant transplantation had failed.

Some time later Morgan recalled that the shipping bill for

Peterson's Butte, Linn County, where pheasants were released in 1882 (Courtesy Oregon State Game Commission)

this fiasco had been around $300, all out of Denny's own pocket. A good many people seeing such a sum down the drain would have called another expedition throwing good money after bad, but the Dennys were convinced that the deed could be done—and would be worth the cost. The trouble, they reassured themselves, had all been in the trans-shipping from Olympia down to Portland—that and not having enough females to insure successful broods. Well, then, they would profit by experience. They had been warned that the ringnecks were independent, freedom-loving and would fight the caging, but they had not realized how fiercely their longing for liberty burned.

This time Owen found space on a vessel sailing direct to Portland, the barque *Isle of Bute*. No cramming into crates for this band. Owen had an enormous cage constructed amidships, some twenty feet high and equally wide, with tall bamboo as real as growing trees for the bars, a whole scow-load of gravel for the floor, and there were tubbed seedlings round-about to add to the semblance of freedom, the familiarity of homeland thicket. Plenty of grain for feed was stored nearby, and the tubbed seedlings would furnish the daily ration of greenery that seemed so all-important for pheasant good health. For their good digestion's sake, there was charcoal sacked handily nearby, too. Most important of all, arrangements had been made for Owen's brother John to release these birds on Peterson Butte, right behind the Denny homestead, where family and neighbors could protect them from over-ardent "shootists."

Gertrude was every bit as eager for pheasants in Oregon as her husband. On March 26, 1882, she wrote a letter home to her sister-in-law, Mrs. William Ralston:

Owen has sent a lot more things to John, fine breeds of chickens, ducks, etc. and some of those pheasants to be turned out on the butte there back of Mother Denny's place. He thinks that perhaps the folks there will protect them for the sake of the Denny family, till they get a good start in the country. I hope they will, for they are splendid eating and they are a beautiful bird and large size. After they get started they will scatter out. I hope they will get out into the mountains beyond Roseburg where they won't be hunted so much till they get to be plenty. Owen sent home lots of trees and plants, too. Melvin* is going to take care of them till we come and of course he will have some of them for his trouble. The things ought to be there before this time.

Sailing across the Pacific in the 1880s was not always a matter of arrival dates calculated to the dot, but this time Gertrude was right. The second band of pioneer pheasants had arrived before her letter, for the *Isle of Bute* made harbor March 13. The *Oregonian*, still resolute in chronicling *Mongolian* pheasants in keeping with its own first misstatement, cited the event on March 19 (p. 1, col. 7):

The Mongolian pheasants and Chinese partridges brought hither by the barque Isle of Bute were brought ashore last Monday and turned out to become naturalized Oregonians. Their habitat is known to us, but we suppress it for reasons that have a bearing upon the field shooting of the dulcet hereafter. Ten years from now no swell dinner will be complete without them, thanks to Judge Denny of Shanghai.

And thanks to John Denny of Lebanon and his family, nephews and neighbors, the birds were given good welcome and no bother made if they sensibly chose to forage in the chicken yard for a few days before they ventured into the wild. They would not choose to stay barnyard birds, Owen had predicted. The freedom-loving nature of both cock and hen would soon impel them to range afar, and the cocks' springtime renewal of the urge to claim harem rights and harem territory would complete the dispersion.

This time there were more hens than cocks. Just how many more is not certain. When William B. Shaw of Washington State College at Pullman interviewed Gertrude and her daughter Nettie in 1908 for his book, *The China or Denny Pheasant in Oregon*, he reported their recollection that thirty birds had been shipped and all but four arrived alive. But a good many other collectors of pheasant data report twenty-eight survivors out of "over thirty" shipped, and those are the figures mentioned by Owen in a letter to the Massachusetts Game Commission.** The number of survivors has also

* The typed copy of the letter in Oregon Historical Society files reads Melvin. John's son was named Malcolm; is this an error? The son seems likely meant.

** The letter is published in the Massachusetts Game Commission report of 1894, p. 17, and is cited by Henry Oldys in his *Pheasant Raising in the United States*, U.S. Dept. of Agriculture *Farmers Bulletin 390* (Washington, 1910).

Some of the pheasants the Dennys sent to Oregon traveled in wicker baskets like this one
(Courtesy Oregon State Game Commission)

been given as twenty-five and twenty-seven. The differences
are too small to be of much concern, and all seem to agree
that there were ten cocks.

Ten cocks with fifteen to eighteen hens for the taking now
found themselves with at least a wife or two apiece, and they
all settled down in proper pheasant pattern. Some of the
pairs or trios stayed close to the cage that John Denny had
left with open door and scattered grain on Peterson Butte —
Washington Butte, it had been called before pioneer Asa Pe-

terson came along to settle nearby. Others roamed farther
afield, and a pair was reportedly seen fifty miles away only
two months after arrival. That is farther than pheasants
usually roam unless impelled by great hunger, fear or over-
crowding, but the next year did find pheasants crossing county
lines. Farmers who hadn't yet heard of the foreign imports
rubbed their eyes in amazement at first sight of the bright-
hued strangers, and talk spread till every crossroads store and
town barbershop had its tales of "those birds the Judge sent"
... "those China birds" ... "Chinks" ... "the Denny pheasants" ... and, of course, "the Mongolians."

Meanwhile, Owen had earned home leave, and he and Gertrude returned to Portland for a quick visit in October of
1882, delighted to see how well their second hardy band was
thriving. But there was still danger that "shootists" would
even keep this number from permanent survival. Game was
often scarce in winter and what went into the cook pots de-
pended on what was easiest come by. The birds were spreading out too far now for Owen to be able to rely on the good
faith of just his neighbors. Statewide legislation was needed
to protect the pheasants, Owen argued, and on October 24,
1882, with the help of his old friend Judge Warren Truitt,
Owen saw the legislature's bill prohibiting the taking or killing of pheasants for five years approved by the governor. The
fifty to $100 penalty was stiff enough to make it stick, and
when the Dennys returned to the Orient they had Truitt's
promise that he would get the five-year ban extended if the
birds needed it. He kept his word—and the pheasants got
another six years of protection in a bill passed in 1885, post-
poning legal hunting till November 22, 1891.*

But the Dennys were not ones to do things halfway, and
so they made a third shipment of pheasants, a shipment of
which all record has been lost. Here again we have to count on
memories jogged to recollection long after the events oc-
curred, especially the memory of George Himes, who wrote of
a memorial to Denny and his pheasants in an *Oregonian* article of March 27, 1907 (p. 8, col. 5). Himes' story is that this

---

* See *General Laws of Oregon, 1882*, p. 61; *General Laws of Oregon,
1885*, pp. 5, 29.

additional band of birds—perhaps the second attempt at transplantation instead of the third—was loaded on a steamer San Francisco-bound and addressed to the personal care of the city's mayor. By strange mischance, the mayor died just as the ship docked, and in the overburden of grief and concern surrounding the funeral, no one was delegated to accept the feathered consignment. By the time inquiries were made, the birds had vanished without a trace, although certain persons supposedly reported that some of the ship's crew would smack their lips whenever roast pheasant happened to be mentioned. Like the Lost Colony of Roanoke, these particular pheasant pioneers would offer more to legend than to history.

In autumn of 1884 Owen and Gertrude decided to leave the consular service and return to Portland for good, booking passage early enough so that they would arrive in plenty of time for Christmas. All sorts of Oriental treasures went into the bags, boxes, bundles and baskets that were stored in the hold with the Denny label. There had to be Christmas gifts for all the family, for neighbors and friends, too, and of course they wanted to bring back some of the lovely things they had collected for their home in Shanghai—porcelain vases, teakwood screens, inlaid cabinets, figurines of gold and ivory, silks, painted scrolls.

There were also pheasants, some ninety of them, lodged in seven crates and thirty baskets. A few ringnecks were among the ninety, for the bird with the white torque ring and warlord mien would always be a Denny favorite. But this species was already well established in Linn County and spreading promisingly beyond its borders, and so the Dennys hopefully added five new pioneers: golden pheasants, silver pheasants and tragopans from China, and the green pheasants and copper pheasants of Japan.

Thirty-one of the new band were goldens, for this strikingly beautiful bird of brilliant scarlet-and-gold plumage would surely be a handsome wanderer in western woodlands. Just how many of the remaining fifty-nine or sixty birds were the shorter-tailed tragopans, the silvers, greens, coppers and ringnecks was apparently never recorded, although the *Oregonian* reported their homecoming with a December 15, 1884 article (p. 3, col. 2) headed "Arrival of Chinese Game Birds":

Judge O. N. Denny who arrived here from China by the last steamer brought with him 30 baskets and 7 crates of Chinese game birds. They comprise six varieties of the pheasant family, only four out of about 90 birds having died on the 7,000 mile voyage. Thirty-one are goldens, not one of which died, although the most delicate.

The remainder are silver, copper, green, tragopans and ringnecks, there being only a few of the latter, of which Denny already shipped several at other times and are doing well. Some of the silvers were bred in confinement, but the others were all taken in the wild. A portion of them will be presented to the Multnomah Rod and Gun Club for distribution. These birds have been acclimated in England, France and Germany.

Getting "acclimated" in Portland that cold December day in 1884 was a shivery problem for those eighty-six survivors. Snow so early in the season was not only unexpected, it was almost unheard of in Portland, and here was a regular blizzard whipping along the Willamette, howling across the docks and the huddle of riverfront buildings. The members of the Multnomah Rod and Gun Club—who had been practically seeing those long-tailed birds in their gunsights, almost tasting roast pheasant on their tongues—hurriedly arranged for pheasant shelter. A 50x100-foot room in a downtown building seemed a likely spot and the huntsmen dashed about collecting tubbed evergreens, palms, bamboo—whatever greenery could be begged, pirated or borrowed for pheasant comfort and a disguise of prison walls.

The pheasants were not fooled, they were not comforted. They scratched listlessly in the sand-covered floor, pecked at the tossed grain with half appetite, cast furtive eye at the gray sky and swirling snow framed in the high, narrow windows. Something had to be done.

A few of the birds were taken by some of the gun club members or other friends for home barnyard sanctuary, and the name of at least one such rescuer—Millard Townsend of Lafayette, Yamhill County—was recorded when an interview with Mrs. Denny was published in the *Oregonian*, June 6, 1901. Meanwhile, the prisoners became such a troublesome problem that the men who had them in charge were later sure that there must have been at least 150 birds and thirteen different kinds, instead of the eighty or so, six-fold assortment the unharassed reporter had tallied on the birds' arrival.

Frank T. Dodge seemed to be the member assigned to solve the pheasant difficulty. He had business connections with the Oregon Railway and Navigation Company and through them arranged transportation for the prisoners to a temporary home on Protection Island in Puget Sound, where a mild climate would grant freedom to roam at liberty and the surrounding expanse of water would ensure that the liberty would not take them beyond retrievable bounds. The club committee looked over the island with its 700 acres of untouched wilderness broken only by the home and small garden plot of one lonely settler—a Mr. Powers—noted that there were no owls, no hawks, no vermin to prey on the birds, and voted to a man that Protection Island was well named, the perfect pheasant haven. They also voted Mr. Powers a monthly fee of $25 to look after his new neighbors. Come spring, of course, they'd be shipped back to Oregon for permanent resettling.

Back in Portland the Multnomah Rod and Gun Club treasurer balanced his books one fall day in 1885 and discovered the amount on hand was less than nothing. Nobody seemed disposed to dig into his own pocket to keep the club operating, and so it was disbanded. Mr. Powers wrote about his fees . . . and wrote . . . and wrote.

How many cocks, how many hens, how many silvers, goldens, greens, coppers, tragopans or ringnecks were in Powers' care has never been recorded, but there must have been close to eighty birds on that little island, and if even a third were hens, there must have been a good twenty-five broods hatching in thicket and briar patch as spring turned into summer. Twenty-five broods, with six, eight, ten, even up to fifteen chicks per brood—all unchallenged by preying owl, hawk, raccoon, skunk or barnyard cat—could add up to quite a lot of pheasants. Powers, who must have looked at the first little downy puffball arrivals with a gleam of pride, soon began eyeing the lot with apprehension. When they invaded his garden, feasting on tender shoots of lettuce, on the new carrots, turnips and parsnips he planned to save for his own winter larder, apprehension turned to anguish. How could he get rid of those birds?

Mr. Powers' anguished look turned to hopeful glint. He could convert the island to a private hunting club . . . charge a fee. Would the shootists from nearby Tacoma, Seattle, and British Columbia pay $25 for a chance to get these foreign birds in their gunsights? Would they! The answer was an enthusiastic cheer from the hunters—and a startled reappraisal of their safety by the pheasants.

It was four miles to the nearest land, about four times farther than a pheasant usually flies without resting, but their pinions were strong, their instinct for survival still stronger. They could even swim if they had to, head bobbing with every stroke, and some of the birds reached their goal. Some flew north and took refuge on Vancouver Island to become the first Canadian pheasant pioneers; others went south, keeping to the valleys and foothills, perhaps even crossing the Columbia slough to Oregon. Like Oregon pioneers, the pheasants had enemies to outwit: prowling cats and farmers' dogs, if they strayed too near the settlements. All sorts of four-foot prowlers, if they kept to the wild, and winged predators besides, hawks by day and owls by night. There were also rain and cold, hunger, instinct's ever-constant demand to fill familiar pattern, even when there was nothing of the old way left for starting point. As spring brought the sexual urge on full tide, the cocks took what hens they found for harem complement—those of their own kind if they were available, or any alien conquest that seemed of familiar size and feathering, ruffed grouse, spruce grouse, blue grouse or sharp-tail.

The hybrid offspring of these mesalliances could not reproduce their kind, but they could certainly jolt Washington hunters who thought they'd seen every kind of game bird in the Cascades a dozen times over. Many an oldtimer must have rubbed his eyes and blamed the startling apparition on failing vision—or perhaps too many swigs from a certain jug. At least some of the bewildered beholders thought to get photographic proof, and these pictures would eventually be published in Oregon game commission reports. Meanwhile the pheasants were shifting for themselves as best they could.

No accurate trace was made of their wanderings, and though here and there a count was made and tally recorded of so many coppers, so many greens, goldens or silvers or tragopans, the full story can never be told.

Owen and Gertrude Denny must have heard this tale of wandering with heavy hearts, but there was nothing they could do about it, for they were no longer near at hand in Portland. Although they had firmly said that they were coming home for good, they hadn't even guessed that Owen would be honored with an invitation to become official adviser to the king of Korea. He had refused at first, but the cabled messages kept coming into Portland begging him to reconsider, and he finally acceded.

They had returned in mid-December of 1884. By mid-December of 1885 they were on their way to Seoul, once more to make a home in the Orient, to collect embroidered silks and painted porcelains, carved ivory, jade, teak and sandalwood. But they collected no more pheasants for pioneer transplant.

For one reason, Owen found that his new position was exceedingly complicated and left him little time for following personal whims. Then, too, he was struggling to keep out of court intrigue, to keep out of embroilment with the disputes between China and Korea. Some of his feelings on the matter boiled over into a published pamphlet, *China and Korea,* printed by Kelly and Walsh, Ltd. in Shanghai, 1888. Gertrude was equally involved with court social life, with need for tact and diplomacy and smiling presence, whatever her own inner feelings might be. Life at the Korean court was exciting, challenging—even rewarding—but there was no time for collecting more pheasants. Besides, they had spent quite a sum on the four transplants. "Thousands," Gertrude said once, according to a newspaper interview in 1919.* Another newspaperman, Lester Halpin, re-telling the pheasant chronicle for a feature article in the *Oregonian* Sunday magazine section, December 1, 1935, put the estimated cost at $4,500.

But of course the real reason why the Dennys made no more pheasant shipments was that the ringnecks themselves

---

* Clipping dated July 6, 1919, in Scrapbook 85, p. 119, Oregon Historical Society.

were taking care of their own propagation quite satisfactorily. None of the other breeds had multiplied to the point where they could be called of game-bird quantity, but those ringnecks! By 1888 farmers were beginning to complain that the birds were a misery instead of a boon, that they not only came to glean the volunteer grain along the fence rows, but trod down the ripening stands to midfield depth, and what was worse, the cocks descended upon the chickenyards like Ghengis Khan himself, whipped the startled roosters to a frazzle and took *droit de seigneur* with the hens, bold as bold.

The U.S. Department of Agriculture heard the complaints and sent a representative out to Oregon to investigate—the widely known and highly respected ornithologist, Dr. C. Hart Merriam. Merriam talked to farmers, hunters, asking what kinds of pheasants they had seen, how many, where, when— trying to solve the mystery of the missing Green farm group as well as trace the roving wanderers from Protection Island. He also made careful observations of his own, and so there are both fact and hearsay in his summary published as part of the official U.S. Department of Agriculture *Annual Report* for 1888.*

You can sort out the facts Merriam collected and look at them like the jumbled pieces of a jigsaw puzzle whose picture would portray the pheasant saga. Like most well-used puzzles, it has missing pieces, and you can only guess what fills the gaps. One of the gaps in the pheasant picture is caused by Merriam's statement that there were *four* flourishing pheasant colonies in 1888: one at the south end of Vancouver Island near Victoria, a second on Protection Island, a third at the junction of the Willamette and Columbia, a fourth in the mid-Willamette Valley. The fourth represented the 1882 Peterson Butte pioneers. The first two were the 1884 Washington wanderers. But whence came the Columbia colony? The only pheasants released there had been that original pilgrim band of 1881, all of which had supposedly vanished. Had there been survivors after all, too wary and wily to be detected when Owen's friends made winter search?

* Page 485ff. Merriam's "Sophie Id." is Sauvie Island, and he uses Washington Butte for Peterson Butte.

The question will probably never be fully answered unless some letter or journal of 1882 comes to light with eye-witness chronicle of pheasant survival. Merriam in 1888 could only note that those he questioned said they had seen birds on Sauvie Island and the mainland that first winter, and he does not document any subsequent sightings.

The Columbia colony could have been a new group, founded by rovers from the 1882 band moving north or from the Protection Island birds wandering south. However, this solution would indicate a continuous spread of flocks, a merging, and Merriam definitely speaks of a merger as a future possibility, not present fact. The group might also represent rovers from the 1884 birds released in Yamhill County, for several were seen around Forest Grove, Astoria and elsewhere, but these places are not at the junction of the Willamette and Columbia by quite a few miles. The question is still unanswered: were there survivors of the first pheasant pioneer band that wintered through to establish succeeding generations of Oregon-born birds? Are the Sauvie Island birds on George Green's farm the real first successful pheasant pioneers, or do the Peterson Butte ringnecks get the honor?

Whether or not the Peterson Butte birds were first to survive may be in question, but there is no doubt that they were the hardiest band, the most prolific, the most bent on becoming ancestors of a thriving Oregon-born pheasant population, progenitors of sturdy game bird stock. They were all ringnecks, and as Merriam noted, ringnecks were everywhere most numerous. Of the others only the goldens and the greens were found in any numbers. The tally for coppers, silvers and tragopans could practically be counted on the fingers. No game possibilities there.

Merriam's report was the first official government survey of pheasant status in America, but it was not really prepared from a game bird standpoint, for the Oregon law still prohibited pheasant hunting or trapping of any kind. As Merriam noted, a good many Oregonians were beginning to think that further protection of pheasants was sheer nonsense. Undoubtedly quite a few irate farmers took the law into their own hands and held a "necktie party" for the pheasants, just

as oldtime westerners had done for cattle rustlers and horse
thieves. Uncountable pheasants were likely "mistaken" for
ducks, geese, grouse and other lawful game, too, so that one
way or another Oregonians got a pretty good idea of just how
delicious roast pheasant could be long before the law made
the China birds fair game.

Among the early screamers for repeal of pheasant protection was Theodore T. Geer, later elected governor of Oregon.
Geer introduced an act in the legislature repealing that pro-
tecting the pheasants, and aired his complaints in the January 30, 1889 *Oregonian*. If the repeal were passed, he stated,
pheasants would still be afforded the same protection by state
game laws as "all other birds of similar nature." The birds
were multiplying, he felt, according to the "original biblical
injunction, and are striving, in season and out, for first money.
. . . You had just as well provide for the prevention of the ex-
termination of grasshoppers. . . . I am a friend to the Mongolian Pheasants, and willingly favor giving them the same protection afforded our other birds, but where they are numerous
enough to destroy grain fields it certainly ought to be lawful
to kill them, and in those sections of the State where there
are none it is not at all likely many will be killed."

Repeal was not forthcoming, but the six-year renewal
passed in 1885 did come to an end. The count couldn't have
been accurate to the last bird, but oldtimers used to say that
at least fifty thousand birds were taken the first day pheasant hunting became legal. The first official count of a legal
pheasant season in Oregon was submitted by H. D. McGuire
in his *Report of the Fish and Game Protector, 1893-94*. Mc-
Guire recommended (p. 6) that the closed season for ringnecked pheasants be extended to September 1; that killing of
all other varieties of imported pheasants except the ringnecked be prohibited; and that it be made legal to ship live
pheasants out of state (pp. 18-19). He noted that the special
protection given pheasants in Jackson and Josephine coun-
ties by an 1893 act was having the desired effect, and that the
birds were increasing in the Rogue River region.

Thirteen thousand birds were killed in Linn County alone
in 1893. Market sale (at $1.50 per dozen) was both legal and

profitable, and editor Harvey Scott of the *Oregonian* cried out in protest: "This is not sport. It is butchering as a business."*

Further details were added by McGuire's report for 1895-96, and now for the first time Oregon sent out breeding birds in answer to pleas from every corner of the continent.** Names of receivers and number of birds sent are included in the game reports as full proof that Denny's birds were going to have descendants coast to coast, and those who suggested that the birds be rechristened "Denny pheasants" had good cause.

Just what to call these far-come China birds was very much the concern of L. P. W. Quimby, Oregon State Game and Forestry Warden. In his report for 1899 (pp. 6-8) he called them Mongolians; but in his 1900 report (pp. 14-15), he makes special plea that the Mongolian misnomer be wiped out, for no birds of that species had yet been introduced into the United States. The Oregon Game Commission eventually would do so in 1924, hoping that these birds from more northerly regions would winter better than the ringnecks across the Cascades in eastern Oregon. Yet in 1900 when Quimby wrote so forthrightly of Mongolian misnomer, a misnomer it surely was. Quimby also included pictures of vanishing tragopans, goldens, greens, and other Washington wanderers to make this report of special value for pheasant pioneer record.

Pheasants were abundant, and Frank Wire, later game commissioner, recalled taking eighty-five birds in one day along Soap Creek in Benton County. But the time had to come when abundance was ancient history.

The first limiting of pheasant hunting in Oregon began in the year 1901 when a legal take of ten birds per day was imposed. Birds of either sex were so scarce by 1910 that the Game Commission barred all pheasant shooting both that year and the next. Again, something had to be done about pheasants if the people of Oregon were to continue enjoying both sight and taste of their handsome adoptee.

* June 23, 1894, p. 4.

** In 1896, 634 birds were shipped to "nearly every section of the Union" (p. 86). Among the consignees were James J. Hill and Joaquin Miller. Over the years many pheasants were shipped also to Homer Davenport, whose early pheasant sketches are now at OHS (Drake Collection).

Closed seasons, prohibition of marketing, bag limits and development of wildland refuges for nesting were part of the answer. Even more important was the establishment of a game breeding farm near Corvallis which began breeding operation under state supervision in 1911. Later another farm was set up near Hermiston, and across the land other states followed Oregon's lead in establishing pheasant farms to augment natural population. The full account of the hows and whys of captive pheasant breeding is given in *Pheasant Raising in the United States*, by Henry Oldys (U.S. Department of Agriculture *Farmers Bulletin 390*). Its historical data is drawn largely from the Oregon Game Commission reports and the Merriam survey of 1888 and adds little new material, but many a gun club and state game warden conned this little pamphlet eagerly in the days when pheasant farms were big —and welcome—news.

Gene M. Simpson was the Oregon game farm's first superintendent, and as he began pheasant distribution over the countryside, the farm truck with its load of crates became a familiar sight. The number of farm birds released to the wild has increased year by year to an amazing total. In an article published in the Oregon State Game Commission *Bulletin* (June, 1961), R. U. Mace notes that 1,415, 582 birds were released in Oregon over the preceding fifty years. The two farms at Corvallis and Hermiston can count on having some twenty to thirty thousand birds for release each year, but since Oregon hunters carry home about half a million pheasants as autumn trophies, there's still a lot left up to the pheasants themselves.

Normally, pheasants nest only once each year, and each hen lays eight to fifteen eggs of the same dun hue as the dried grass and soft feathers from her breast that make nest lining and camouflage. Ten or twelve is the usual clutch. All twelve may hatch if the spring isn't unusually cold and damp and the egg-eating crows, magpies, jays, squirrels, weasels, minks, skunks and raccoons, cats and dogs haven't discovered the hideaway. All twelve chicks, however, do not often grow to maturity. A fourth or a half is more likely. Pheasants, like any wildling, live too much on the prongs of danger to allow the raising of a full brood to become a normal event. Often all twelve succumb to the many forms death takes in the wild, and then the hen and cock begin the courtship all over again and in another fortnight there are more eggs for incubation, probably fewer this time. If that brood is also destroyed, they will make a third trial, compelled by instinctive force to complete the ordained pattern of survival. However, if only one chick escapes death, the hen will tend it with all the care and devotion she would have lavished on the entire twelve and not feel compulsion to nest again.

Gamekeepers who have discovered this facet of pheasant behavior often say regretfully that it proves the birds do not know how to count. Consequently the arithmetic of supplying sufficient birds for the autumn open season becomes the game warden's responsibility and he will cruise the fields each spring and fall counting the number seen, estimating how many cocks the farms will have to release to make the hunter's quota.

Owen Denny did not live to see establishment of the game farms, but he was back in Oregon in time for the first hunting season and very much interested in this final phase of his pheasant experiment. He and Gertrude had packed their multitude of boxes and baggage again in January of 1891 and booked around-the-world homeward passage across Asia, Greece and Europe to arrive in Portland in mid-July. They would not return to the Orient. This time the homecoming was really for good.

A house in Portland was necessary for business reasons, but they also began looking around at farms for sale. Owen Denny had never got over being an Oregon farm boy. His brother John now owned the old homestead in Linn County and had added to its acreage, and so Owen invested in eastern Oregon ranch land. Their city home was at 261 Thirteenth, and Owen left there each day to attend to his duties as newly-appointed receiver for the Portland Savings Bank.

Pictures of these years show that the dark, curly hair was not quite so thick as it had once been above Owen's high forehead, but the mustache was still worn with jaunty air, the eyes still shone bright. In 1892 he served as state senator for

Owen N. and Gertrude Hall Denny (OHS Collections)

Multnomah County. Down on the ranch he liked to pitch in with the work whenever he could, but in the late 1890s a bout with a bad-tempered bull resulted in injuries that kept him pretty much on retired status. In 1899 he suffered a paralytic stroke from which he only partially recovered, but he refused to let anything make him a housebound invalid. In June of 1900 he and Gertrude went to Long Beach, up on the Washington Coast, hoping that the change to sea air would be welcome tonic. There the two of them could sit on the verandah and look out across the Pacific and talk of old days in Tientsin . . . in Shanghai . . . at the royal court in Seoul . . . all the to-do about shipping those pheasants.

Owen died there in Long Beach on June 30, 1900, and was brought home for burial. The end had been sudden, peaceful, a release from suffering. Gertrude Denny faced this new sorrow as she had faced old ones—with outer grace and inner grief. It was much easier for her to handle sorrow in those years alone than all the myriad involvements of financial matters. It was so long since she had had to make important decisions by herself. Owen's brother, John, who had shared in the pheasant introduction plans, died also, July 5, 1912, and Gertrude was more alone than before. For both Owen and John the newspapers carried full stories. For Owen there was chronicle of diplomatic posts and legal career; for John an accounting of his role as pioneer, as veteran of the Indian wars in Oregon's Company F, as public-spirited citizen; for both there had been a retelling of the pheasant transplantation, then still very much a matter of Oregon pride. Denny and pheasant were synonymous in Oregon. You could scarcely mention one without the other.

The pheasant pilgrimage usually came in for retelling each time Gertrude Denny's name appeared in the newspapers, too, as the years went on. Each May near her birthday or in November as the anniversary date of the famous Whitman Massacre came around, she would be interviewed and photographed as one of the last—eventually the very last—survivor of that day. Reporters eager for color and something different to add to the old tale, often worked in her recollections of the Orient, how it felt to be a lady at the royal court in Korea, how she and Owen happened to think of sending pheasants to Oregon. In 1901 she tried to get the Protection Island pheasants returned to Oregon, but a gun club had bought the island and although the *Oregonian* published her plea in the June 6 issue, no action was taken. Probably none was possible.

Gertrude liked to remember, to talk about the old days, but the time came when she could no longer brighten the interviews by letting the reporters see and touch the Oriental treasures she and Owen had gathered with so much pleasure. She had had to sell them one by one to eke out her meager funds and most of them had gone to an apparently unscrupulous dealer who had paid far less than their worth. She had accepted the small price he offered, thinking—no doubt— only of the few dollars she had paid for them in Shanghai's street of shops or in Seoul markets, not of all the shipping costs that had added to their value, the breakage toll that would make one vase arriving unbroken out of three she had packed increase to triple worth. "She no longer owns her famous set of three gold inlaid cabinets, and her handcarved vases and oriental bricabrac," one reporter noted regretfully in a January 23, 1919* account of Whitman survivors. Sportsmen who read of her plight bethought themselves of all the hours of pleasure they had had, following the pheasant over autumn hills, seeing the cock's burst of jewel-tone glory against the sky, and they pledged themselves to obtain for her a widow's pension from the pheasant hunting fees. After all, it was she as much as Owen who had given the pheasants to Oregon. The pension would be only just return.

There was no argument on the matter, but legal action took time and in the interim some of the Oregon sportsmen put their hands in their own pockets to see that she had some of the little extra comforts a woman of eighty enjoys. Her daughter Nettie would never let her really go in want, of course, but to independent Gertrude Denny there was nothing quite like having money of her own. And it did seem money rightfully hers when on July 6, 1919, she was paid the

____

* Clipping in Scrapbook 85, p. 106, OHS.

first fifty-dollar installment of a pension that could run up to $1,200.

"I ought to celebrate," Gertrude said happily.

Her daughter Nettie twinkled back at her. "Something wild," she approved. "Real wild."

Gertrude thought a minute. "I guess," she decided, "I'll just have all the ice cream I can eat!"

On a hot July day that seemed fitting celebration. Not "wild" perhaps—unless she gobbled it down and got a stomach ache—but good fun and practical at the same time. Just like Gertrude, Owen would have said. He would have been pleased to know that the pheasants he had sent were giving her the treat. Owen had not quite reached his sixty-second birthday when death came in 1900. When Gertrude died on August 5, 1933, she was well past ninety-six.

"Sometimes I feel as if I had lived two hundred years!" she had once told a reporter, and the kind, motherly face clouded for a moment, losing its accustomed brightness. The reporter had laughed, but looking back at Gertrude's story of pioneer journey . . . the massacre seen with a ten-year-old's horror-filled eyes . . . frontier hardships . . . the sudden death of her firstborn, her only son . . . a divorce in days when such action often brought social ostracism for a woman . . . remarriage . . . homemaking in Oregon, Tientsin, Shanghai, Seoul. . . . It did add up to a lot of living.

And the pheasants? Their pioneer chronicle has to be written with many turns and twists, too. But they did adapt to the new land, they did become fully naturalized Oregonians as Owen and Gertrude had hoped. With the aid of game laws and game farms they have become fully American as well, known in almost all of the fifty states. These American pheasants are of predominantly ringneck strain, but not purely so. Three other races within the genus *Phasianus* have also found foothold on American soil—the blackneck, the Kirghiz-Mongolian and the green—and all of these have interbred with the ringneck to add their color shadings to his in modification of the American pheasant pattern. In England, too, the ringneck and green have been introduced to vary the old strain. Of late years only the Kirghiz-Mongolian and the ringneck have been imported here in the States as pure strain birds to add to the native wildling mixture, and both give the American bird the typical torque of white to keep the name of "ringnecked pheasant" in common speech.

However, here and there where birds of blackneck ringless ancestry have been introduced, pheasants without the name-sake white collar can still be seen. In time, perhaps the American strain will stabilize itself with reproduced pattern that remains the same year after year, not quite like any of those already classified in the systematists' record. If that time comes, there are surely justifiable grounds for suggesting that the Denny name be Latinized as substitute for Old World *torquatus* in commemoration of pioneer sponsoring.

Meanwhile, the pheasants themselves make their own un-marked memorial. Downy chicks in early summer, gangly poults and cockerels come fall, soft-feathered brown hens and resplendent roosters all year 'round bear silent witness to honor the Denny name, even though it is not written where all who look may read. Public School Number Seventy-Eight in Lebanon, Oregon, bears the Denny name and a huge bill-board sign proclaims that the ringnecked pheasant—what else?—is the school mascot. But elsewhere the once-familiar phrase of "Denny pheasant" has all but slipped from the tongue, and even the accounts that credit Oregon with pheas-ant pioneering do not often mention the names of Owen and Gertrude Denny.

The facts are set down now for all who find satisfaction in knowing even the small twists on history's trail . . . for all who take to the woods with field-glass or gun . . . all who find beauty in nature's ways. The soft acorn-mottling of a pheas-ant hen, the cock's blue-black plumicorns above hooked beak and crimson cheek armor, white neck chain and jeweled bronze plumage will always serve reminder that the Denny name and the pheasants' pioneer journey belong together in Oregon chronicle.